Countries Around the World

Lithuania

Melanie Waldron

Heinemann Library
Chicago, Illinois

www.heinemannraintree.com
Visit our website to find out more information about Heinemann-Raintree books.

To order:
☎ Phone 888-454-2279
🖥 Visit www.heinemannraintree.com to browse our catalog and order online.

Edited by Kate de Villiers and Vaarunika Dharmapala
Designed by Joanna Hinton-Malivoire
Original illustrations © Capstone Global Library Ltd 2011
Illustrated by Oxford Designers & Illustrators
Picture research by Ruth Blair
Originated by Capstone Global Library Ltd
Printed and bound in China by CTPS

15 14 13 12 11
10 9 8 7 6 5 4 3 2 1

Library of Congress Cataloging-in-Publication Data
Waldron, Melanie.
  Lithuania / Melanie Waldron.
    p. cm.—(Countries around the world)
  Including bibliographical references and index.
  ISBN 978-1-4329-5212-9 (hardcover)—ISBN 978-1-4329-5237-2 (pbk.) 1. Lithuania—Juvenile literature. I. Title.
  DK505.23.W3 2012
  947.93—dc22   2010039280

Acknowledgments
We would like to thank the following for permission to reproduce photographs: Alamy p. 14 (© PjrStudio), p. 29 (© F1online digitale Bildagentur GmbH), p. 34 (© SCPhotos); Corbis p. 7 (© Franz-Marc Frei), p. 8 (© Peter Turnley), p. 26 (© INTS KALNINS/ Reuters); Photolibrary p. 18 (Pixtal Images), p. 23 (Ian Trower/ Robert Harding Travel); Shutterstock p. 5 (© tfrisch99), p. 9, 10, 30, 35 (© Birute Vijeikiene), p. 11 (© Ints Vikmanis), p. 13 (© JuliusKielaitis), p. 16 (© Outsider), p. 17 (© hfuchs), p. 19 (© Marcin Tomczak), p. 20 (© Andrea Seemann), p. 25 (© Shmel), p. 31 (© Anna Lurye), p. 32 (© Oleksiy Naumov), p. 33 (© Jonutis), p. 46 (© totolekoala).

Cover photograph of Trakai Castle reproduced with permission of Photolibrary (© Robert Harding Travel).

We would like to thank Daniel Block and Virginija Craig for their invaluable help in the preparation of this book.

Every effort has been made to contact copyright holders of material reproduced in this book. Any omissions will be rectified in subsequent printings if notice is given to the publisher.

Disclaimer
All the Internet addresses (URLs) given in this book were valid at the time of going to press. However, due to the dynamic nature of the Internet, some addresses may have changed, or sites may have changed or ceased to exist since publication. While the author and publisher regret any inconvenience this may cause readers, no responsibility for any such changes can be accepted by either the author or the publisher.

Contents

Some words in the book are in bold, **like this**. You can find out what they mean by looking in the glossary.

Introducing Lithuania

What do you know about Lithuania? For many years Lithuania was a secret place, hardly visited by tourists or businesspeople. For much of its history, it was ruled over by neighboring countries. However, since Lithuania declared **independence** in 1990, it has become a key part of Europe's future.

An emerging nation

Lithuania is one of the three Baltic states, along with Latvia and Estonia. It has a gentle, rolling landscape dotted with **medieval** villages, but there are also huge areas of wilderness untouched by humans. The modern cities are vibrant and full of life. Lithuanian people are proud of their country, and they are happy to welcome people to explore it.

A fascinating beginning

In the 1200s, King Mindaugas united several different tribes who lived in the land now known as Lithuania. The powerful Grand Duke Gediminas, who ruled from 1316 to 1341, extended Lithuania's borders until it became one of the largest states in Europe. So what happened to Lithuania, and why did it lose its power? How does Lithuania's past shape the country today?

How to say...
Hello *Sveiki* (Svay-key)
How are you? *Kaip gyvuojate?* (Kipe gee-vu-o-yah-teh?)
My name is... *Mano vardas yra...* (Mah-noh var-r-dus-ee-rah...)
I'm from... *As esu is...* (Ush ehsoo ish...)
Yes *Taip* (Tipe)
No *Ne* (Neh)

The island castle of Trakai was built for Lithuania's early leaders. It is a beautiful building in an amazing setting.

History: An Occupied Land

In 1386, the grand duke of Lithuania, Jogaila, also became king of Poland. Lithuania remained an independent country, with its own laws and customs. These stayed in place even after the Union of Lublin created a Polish-Lithuanian state in 1569.

In 1795, Russia invaded Lithuania and took it over as part of the huge Russian Empire. Many Lithuanians tried to **revolt**, but they were defeated. In order to stop them from revolting again, the Russians repressed the Lithuanians' society and language. Only Russian, not Lithuanian, was taught in most schools. There was also a ban on printing books in Lithuanian.

A taste of independence

During World War I, Germany invaded Lithuania. The Russian Empire collapsed in 1917, and when Germany was defeated in 1918, Lithuania became independent again. However, this new-found freedom did not last long. In 1940, during World War II, the **communist Soviet Union** invaded the Baltic states. Lithuania became the Lithuanian Soviet Socialist Republic.

From 1941 until 1944, Germany carried out an invasion of the Soviet Union, known as "Operation Barbarossa," and Lithuania was once again invaded by Germany. For Lithuania's **Jews**, this was a disaster. Almost all of Lithuania's 200,000 Jewish citizens were **persecuted** and murdered as part of the **Holocaust**.

FEIGA MALNIK (1905–1944)

Feiga was Jewish and lived in Kovno. She was a beautician, her husband was a barber, and together they ran a shop. In 1941 the Germans forced them to live in the Jewish **ghetto** in Kovno. On October 28, 1941, 10,000 Jews were murdered. Feiga survived, but in 1944 she was deported to a **concentration camp**, where she died.

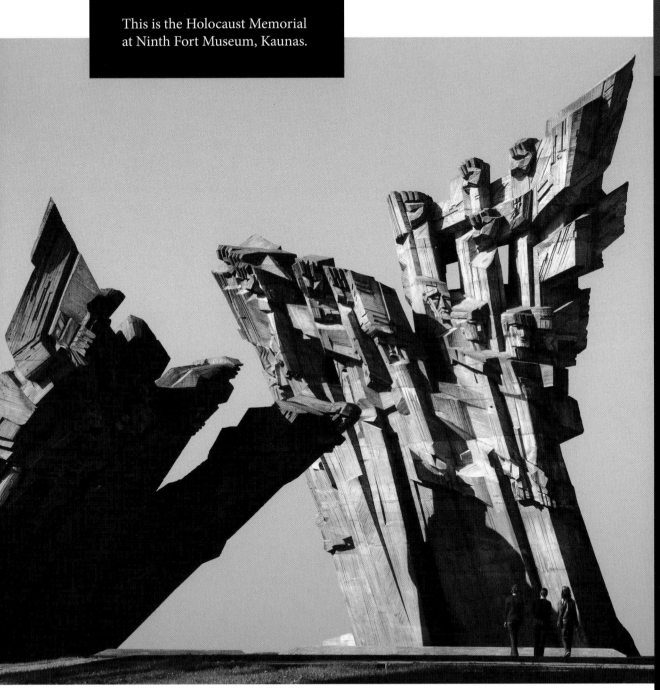

This is the Holocaust Memorial at Ninth Fort Museum, Kaunas.

Modern Lithuania

In 1944, a year before Germany's defeat in World War II, the Soviet Union again took control of Lithuania. Once again, Lithuanians resisted. This time the Soviet response was tougher. Many Lithuanians were **deported** to labor camps in Siberia.

However, during the 1980s, the support for **independence** grew. The Soviet government was also becoming less severe. In 1989, there was a mass protest against Soviet occupation across the Baltic states. Two million people linked hands, creating a human chain 370 miles (600 kilometers) long. Lithuania eventually became independent on September 6, 1991. Less than two weeks later, it joined the United Nations (**UN**). In 2004, it joined the European Union (**EU**) and **NATO**.

Lithuanians and Estonians wave their flags in protest of the Soviet occupation of the Baltic states.

New government, new society

The new government introduced many changes. These led to a more Western-style society, but there were problems to begin with. Jobs were hard to find, and many people were poor. But by the early years of the 21st century, the **economy** had recovered and was booming! This lasted until 2008, when the global economy crashed. Lithuania was hit hard, and unemployment reached 14 percent in 2009. It is slowly recovering.

The people of Lithuania are generally respectful of minority **ethnic groups**. More than the other Baltic states, Lithuania has accepted Russians into its society. However, there is very little Russian-language education or television. There are over 100 different ethnic groups in the country, although most people are Lithuanian. They have held on to Lithuanian culture and traditions throughout their difficult history. Now the new society is looking ahead to the future.

These Lithuanians are enjoying an arts and crafts fair in Vilnius.

Regions and Resources:
The Center of Europe

Lithuania is roughly the same size as the state of West Virginia. It is located on the edge of the Baltic Sea and shares borders with Belarus, Latvia, Poland, and the Russian region of Kaliningrad. It claims to be the center of Europe, and there is a museum and monument to mark this. The capital city, Vilnius, is located in the southeast corner of the country.

Forests and lakes are a common sight in the Lithuanian landscape.

A mixed climate

Lithuania's coastal climate does not vary a huge amount between summer and winter. However, toward the east of the country, where it borders the huge European landmass, there are far greater swings in temperature. Summers are generally warm and wet, and winters can get very cold.

This ice fisherman is walking across a frozen lake.

Daily life
During a harsh winter, the temperature in Vilnius can drop to -13°F (-25°C)! Usually, though, winter temperatures are around 23°F (-5°C), and rarely climb above freezing. Most of the surrounding lakes and rivers freeze over. Some locals enjoy ice-fishing, while many more enjoy sledding down the Bastion hill in Vilnius!

The regions of Lithuania

Lithuania is divided into five different regions:

Aukstaitija

This is the largest region, covering the middle, north, and east. The hilly uplands are covered in beautiful forests, and there are also many lakes. The farms in the region are small, and many are preserved to keep the traditional way of life.

Zemaitija

This region in western Lithuania is the biggest dairy producer for the country. The low, flat land is perfect for grazing cows. The Zemaitija National Park, with its forests and lakes, is a popular tourist spot in summer.

Dzukija

This region in the southeast of the country is an area of beautiful forests, rivers, and tumbling waterfalls. There are also marshlands full of wild flowers and insects. Ancient villages dot the landscape, and the wilderness areas are protected by wildlife and **botanical** reserves.

Suvalkija

This fertile land in the southwest of Lithuania is mainly agricultural, with small farms surrounded by trees. In the southeast part of the region there are hills and the beautiful Lake Vistytis.

Lithuania minor

This is Lithuania's smallest region and includes the coastline. The landscape is gentle and rolling. The most spectacular part of the region is the beautiful Curonian Spit, with its sand **dunes**, forests, and **lagoons**.

This map shows the regions, national parks, and forests of Lithuania.

This is Lake Galve, one of Lithuania's many beautiful lakes.

13

Natural resources

Lithuania's greatest natural resource is its land. The main agricultural products are grain, potatoes, sugar beets, vegetables, beef, milk, and eggs. The large areas of forest produce timber for building and other wood products. Off the coast there is a small fishing industry.

One unusual resource in Lithuania is **amber**, which is found along the coast. Although it is not mined commercially, many people make a living by collecting it and making it into beautiful jewelry and ornaments.

This amber is thought to be about 40 million years old. Can you see the ant trapped inside it?

The land contains some minerals, including clay, quartz, gypsum, and dolomite. There are also areas of limestone and peat. In Lithuania's coastal waters there are small reserves of oil. However, this does not produce enough to meet Lithuania's needs, so oil is also **imported**.

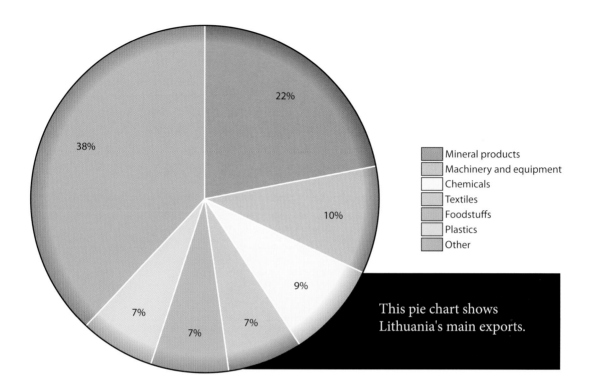

22%

38%

10%

9%

7%

7%

7%

Mineral products
Machinery and equipment
Chemicals
Textiles
Foodstuffs
Plastics
Other

This pie chart shows
Lithuania's main exports.

Industries

Lithuania's location in the center of Europe puts it in a strong position for the future. Modern industries include the transport of goods, including oil and gas to and from Russia. The transport of people is also a growing industry, as more and more Europeans begin to move in and out of the region. The seaport of Klaipeda is the only year-round, ice-free port on the Baltic coast, so a lot of goods pass through it.

New industries such as warehousing are beginning to take over from the older industries of mining and manufacturing. **Biotechnology** and information technology companies are attracting highly qualified people. An increase in tourism is creating many more jobs in the **service industries**. However, in parts of **rural** Lithuania, life and work continue on the land as they have for decades.

Wildlife: Lucky Storks and Shifting Sands

Forests cover a massive 33 percent of Lithuania's total area! The most common tree species are pine, spruce, and birch. Ash and oak have become rare. There are some patches of ancient forest in Aukstaitija National Park, where there are also rare forest plants. The rare ghost orchid can be found here, as can the oldest tree in the country—a 1,500-year-old oak.

These huge areas of forest are home to a host of animals. There are over 70 species of mammals including elk, wild boar, bats, and the **endangered** lynx. There are over 300 species of birds! Insect life is also abundant, with over 600 species of beetles and 640 species of butterflies.

This is the Stelmuze Oak, Lithuania's oldest tree. It is about 1,500 years old.

This beautiful creature is a lynx.

A threat to forest life

Although Lithuania has five national parks (and many regional parks) where the natural habitat is protected, some areas of forest are under threat. Illegal logging is the biggest problem, and is damaging the fragile ecology in some areas. This is a blow to many Lithuanians, who generally have a deep respect for nature. This respect stems from the country's **pagan** days, 600 years ago, when forests were considered **sacred**, and people worshipped them.

How to say...

animal *gyvūnas* (gee-voo-nahs)
bat *šikšnosparnis* (shisksh-noh-spar-niss)
butterfly *drugys* (droo-gees)
ecology *ekologija* (eko-law-gee-yah (g like in geese))
horse *arklys* (ark-lease or ark-lees)
insect *vabzdys* (vabz-dees)
lynx *lūšis* (loo-shis)

A land of lakes

In the last ice age, Lithuania was covered in enormous **glaciers**. These carved out huge pits in the land. When the ice melted, these pits filled with water to become lakes. There are over 4,000 lakes spread across the country, adding much to the beauty of the land.

Some of Lithuania's lakes are home to rare freshwater turtles—but the most spectacular wildlife feature is the huge variety of birds. Black-throated divers, black storks, curlews, and snipes are among the hundreds of species living by the lakes.

Graceful swans make their homes on lakes and lakeshores.

Lake Plateliai is the largest and deepest lake in western Lithuania. It is 4.6 square miles (12 square kilometers) in size and 154 feet (47 meters) deep. There is a beautiful mix of unique plant and animal life in the surrounding forests and marshes. The white water lily, single-leafed bog orchid, and hairy milk vetch are some of the more unusual plants.

Problems with pollution

The Zuvintas Reserve includes Lake Zuvintas and the Bukta Forest. There are important wetlands, with 255 species of birds registered here. But poor water-level controls and pollution from **fertilizers** are damaging the local environment. Plans are now underway to save the reserve.

Daily life

Lithuanians believe that storks bring them good luck. The birds herald the arrival of spring, when every year they fly back from Africa to the same nesting site. Farmers celebrate Stork Day on March 25 by stirring the seeds they will plant that year. This is believed to ensure a good crop.

Infrastructure: Politics, Travel, and Education

After **independence** in 1991, the Republic of Lithuania agreed on its **constitution** in October 1992. This sets out the rights, freedoms, and responsibilities of all Lithuanian citizens.

Shared power

The powers of state are shared among parliament (*Seimas*), the president, the government, and the **judiciary**. These are all based in the capital city, Vilnius.

Seimas: There are 141 elected members. They can make changes to the constitution and make new laws.

President: This post is held for five years, and then a new person is voted in. The president must approve all new laws.

Government : This includes the prime minister and ministers. The government controls the country and its security, and deals with international matters.

Judiciary: This is the country's **legal** system.

This map shows the 10 counties of Lithuania.

This is the Presidential Palace in Vilnius.

DALIA GRYBAUSKAITĖ (1956–)
FIRST WOMAN PRESIDENT

Dalia Grybauskaitė was born in Vilnius. She went to college in Leningrad, where she studied political **economy**. After college she worked as a secretary and then a lecturer, before entering politics. She became president of Lithuania in May 2009, winning a huge share of the votes. She speaks four languages other than Lithuanian—English, Russian, Polish, and French.

Learning the language

Lithuanian is a complex and ancient language, with many regional and local **dialects** and accents. It is a **phonetic** language, so once you know what a letter sounds like, you should be able to pronounce any word! Russian, Polish, and English are also widely spoken in Lithuania.

Traveling in Lithuania

Lithuania's public transportation system is old, but it runs efficiently and does not cost much. Buses are the best way to travel around the country. They link everything from the main cities to remote villages. The train network is not so efficient. The trains are less frequent than buses, and journeys are slower.

There are four international airports in Lithuania: Vilnius, Kaunas, Palanga, and Siauliai. Vilnius has the largest airport, and is the place where most visitors to Lithuania arrive. There are other smaller airports dotted around the country. Klaipeda is the country's only seaport. Huge cruise ships dock here, and passenger and cargo ferries carry goods and people to and from other European ports.

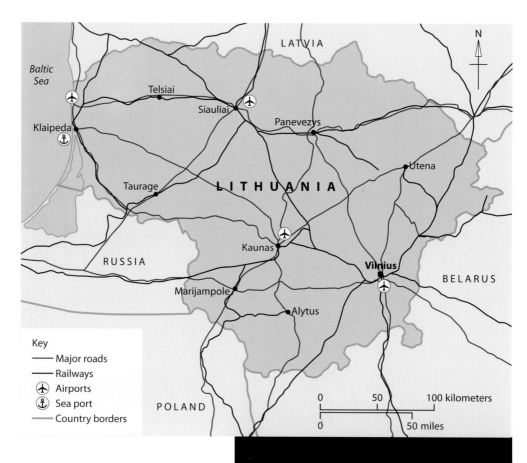

This map shows the major roads, airports, and seaports in Lithuania.

Fast cars and slow carts

The main highways that run through Lithuania are in a good condition and well maintained. The roads in the countryside are a lot more basic! Road traffic ranges from fast and powerful cars, especially in and around the cities, to horses and carts in remote **rural** areas. In winter, many roads become impassable due to heavy snow. Only the main roads are regularly cleared.

Money, money, money

The **currency** in Lithuania is the *litas* (Lt), made up of 100 *centas*. There are around 2.5 *litas* for every U.S. dollar, around 4 *litas* for every British pound, and around 3.5 *litas* for every **euro**. The *litas* is due to be replaced by the euro in 2014.

This is the town of Klaipeda, with its busy seaport in the background.

How to say...
ship *slaivas* (laivas)
train *traukinys* (trow-key-ness)

Education

Young people in Lithuania have a high standard of education. Education is free and **compulsory** between the ages of six and sixteen. There are three levels of schools:

Elementary school (*Pradinė mokykla*) for ages 6–11.

Junior high school (*Pagrindinė mokykla*) for ages 10–17. Pupils have important exams at the end of this stage.

Senior high school (*Vidurinė mokykla*) for ages 16–19. Pupils also have important exams at the end of this stage.

These girls attend a Jewish school in Vilnius.

Students must study a core set of subjects, including Lithuanian, math, history, and a foreign language. In addition, they can choose to study other subjects, such as more languages, science, and art.

Daily life

A typical day at secondary school starts at 8:30 a.m. There are usually six lessons of 45 minutes each. Classes have around 25–30 students each. The lessons end at around 2:10 p.m., but there are usually a lot of different after-school activities offered, such as choir practice or dancing. Most students do homework every evening.

Health care

The health care in Lithuania is provided free. Ambulances and emergency care are very efficient, but some other services suffer from a lack of equipment, medical supplies, and drugs. There is a small amount of private medical care available that offers a better and quicker standard of care. The World Health Organization placed Lithuania 73rd out of 190 countries in its ranking of world health systems in 2000.

How to say...

ambulance *greitosios pagalbos automobilis* (gray-toh-seeos pah-gal-boss aoo-to-mo-be-liss)
school *mokykla* (moo-keek-lah)
education *švietimas* (shvyeh-ti-mahs)
exam *egzaminas* (egg-zah-min-ahs)
hospital *ligoninė* (lee-goh-ni-neh)
health *sveikatas* (svay-kah-tah)

Culture: Folk Music, Jazz, and Festivals

Despite being occupied by other countries for many years, the Lithuanian people have maintained their own culture. At the heart of this culture is folk music, which is usually played on reed instruments, and stringed instruments called *kankles*. Traditional songs (called *dainos*) tell stories of all aspects of life, and are often accompanied by traditional folk dances.

The capital city, Vilnius, was the European Capital of Culture in 2009. The city holds around 30 festivals throughout the year focusing on different aspects of the country's culture—for example poetry, classical music, and dance. In September there is a festival of fire sculpture to celebrate the autumn **equinox**.

Modern sounds

Jazz is hugely popular in Lithuania. After independence, Lithuanian jazz musicians stunned the western music world with their modern free jazz. The Ganelin Trio became world famous. Today, both Kaunas and Vilnius hold yearly jazz festivals where cutting-edge jazz can be heard. There is also a growing pop music scene in Lithuania, but very few groups are known internationally.

YOUNG PEOPLE

Skamp is a pop group that blends pop, hip-hop, and reggae. In 2001 they represented Lithuania at the Eurovision Song Contest, finishing in 13th place. They have supported some international stars, like the Black Eyed Peas and Macy Gray.

These people are dancing at a folk festival in one of Vilnius's parks.

Daily life

Within the old town area of Vilnius lies an area populated by a lot of artists. They have created their own little "breakaway state," which celebrates its "**independence**" day on April Fool's Day! People dress up as border guards and stamp people's passports as they enter the area. The residents have drawn up a **constitution**, in which dogs are given the right to be dogs!

Art, literature, and religion

Many of Lithuania's writers fled the country during the years of occupation, when everything was checked and **censored**. Others stayed, but some of them were imprisoned and tortured. Since independence, writers have been able to express themselves freely and write without fear of **persecution**.

Visual arts

Up until the 1300s, most Lithuanian art was **pagan**, decorative woodcarving. **Fine art** became popular with the spread of the **Christian** religion. Modern art did not take off until the 1950s, when the Soviet government became more relaxed. It is now thriving—along with modern photography, much of which has gained international recognition. Algis Griškevičius is a Lithuanian photographer whose images are famous worldwide.

Religion

Lithuania was the last pagan country in Europe, and only adopted Christianity in 1387. The majority of the population became Roman Catholic, but this religion was suppressed by the **communist Soviet Union** during their years of occupation. Churches were closed or turned into museums—or even radio stations! This only made the religion stronger among Lithuanians, who saw it as a symbol of their struggle for independence.

Over the years, many people have come to pray at the Hill of Crosses near Siauliai. They bring crosses with them to add to the thousands already there.

Food and drink

Traditional Lithuanian food is based on potatoes, meat, and dairy products. In the forested regions, dishes will usually contain mushrooms, berries, and **game**. Fish and seafood is found in coastal regions. Most Lithuanian bread is made from **rye**, and is black in color.

Saltibarsciai (cold beet soup)

Ask an adult to help you make this delicious soup.

Ingredients:

- 2–3 red beets
- 2 medium cucumbers
- 1 tablespoon of chopped chives
- 2 hard-boiled eggs
- 1 cup sour cream
- 1 quart (32 oz) buttermilk
- 1 tablespoon of fresh chopped dill
- a pinch of salt

What to do:

1. Clean, trim, and peel the beets. Cover with water and boil until tender.
2. Peel the cucumbers and chop into small cubes. Peel the eggs and separate the whites from the yolks. Chop the whites very finely. Mash the egg yolks with the chives and the salt.
3. When the beets are tender, remove them from the pan, keeping the liquid.
4. When the beets have cooled, grate them coarsely.
5. In a large bowl, add the buttermilk to 1 quart (32 oz) of the beet water and blend in the sour cream. Then add the beets, cucumber, egg white, and egg yolk mix. Stir well.
6. Chill and garnish with the chopped dill.

Sports and recreation

In Lithuania, almost everyone is passionate about basketball. Many people play, and most people support a team. Lithuania's national team won the bronze medal at the 1992, 1996, and 2000 Olympic games, and just missed out on bronze at the 2004 and 2008 games. The two biggest rival teams in Lithuania are Lietuvos Rytas and Zalgiris Kaunas.

This basketball game is being played between Lithuania and the United States.

SARUNAS MARČIULIONIS (1964-)

Marčiulionis started his basketball career with Statyba Vilnius in 1981. In 1989, he moved to the United States to play professionally for California's Golden State Warriors. After the earthquake in San Francisco in 1989, he helped to pull out passengers trapped in a train while wearing his Warriors shirt. He is now retired.

A range of activities

Lithuania's gentle and **rural** landscape means that there are a lot of different activities to enjoy. Cycling is very popular with both locals and visitors. Horse riding is a growing activity, and in the winter the deep snow is perfect for cross-country skiing.

The numerous lakes dotted across the country provide excellent fishing—as well as more active pastimes like swimming, surfing, sailing, rowing, and canoeing. The beautiful countryside is ideal for hiking and bird-watching, and the forests are excellent hunting grounds for mushroom-picking!

Ice-yachting is a sport that is growing in popularity in Lithuania.

How to say...
basketball *krepšinis* (krap-she-niss)
cycling *dviračiai* (dvee-rah-tiss)
horse riding *raitelis* (rye-tell-iss)
sailing *buriavimas* (boo-ree-ah-vee-mahs)
skiing *slidinėjimas* (slee-dee-neh-yeh-mahs)
swimming *plaukimas* (plow-kee-mahs)

Lithuania Today

Lithuania and its people have had many struggles over the last few hundred years. But despite occupation and invasion, Lithuania has held on to the idea of itself as an independent nation.

The strong cultural traditions of Lithuania are clear for any visitor to see. But Lithuanians are also looking toward the future and working hard to bring the country up to date. This fascinating mix of old and new makes the country an exciting and diverse place to visit.

Modern life

Today, the modern cities in Lithuania are vibrant and sometimes hectic! Fashionable apartments, bars, and restaurants line the streets, and modern offices and fast cars show that business is doing well.

There are many modern shops and restaurants in the Old Town area of Vilnius.

Certainly, there is still work to be done. For example, there are worries about future energy supplies, and the **economy** needs to improve. But crime rates are quite low, health care is free, and the quality of life in Lithuania is generally high. After gaining **independence**, the country is putting its troubled past behind it and is ready to take on the 21st century.

Spread the word!

What Lithuania needs now is **publicity**! It is a small country with a lot to offer visitors. It can offer the excitement of fascinating cities, festivals, and a wide range of sporting and fun activities—or it can offer the opportunity to relax or enjoy wildlife in the beautiful and peaceful countryside. Lithuanians know that their country is unique and special, and they want everyone else to know it, too!

The Kaziukas arts and crafts fair is held every year in Vilnius and attracts tens of thousands of people.

Fact File

Official name:	Republic of Lithuania
Official language:	Lithuanian
Capital city:	Vilnius
Bordering countries:	Belarus, Latvia, Poland, the Russian Region of Kaliningrad
Land area:	25,173 square miles (65,200 square kilometers)
Population:	3,545,319 (July 2010 est.)
Largest cities (population):	Vilnius (560,192) Kaunas (348,624) Klaipėda (182,752) Šiauliai (125,453)
Birth rate:	9.21 births per 1,000 people
Life expectancy (total):	75.12 years
Life expectancy (men):	70.23 years
Life expectancy (women):	80.29 years
Ethnic groups (percentage):	Lithuanian (83.4%) Polish (6.7%) Russian (6.3%) Other (3.6%)
Religion (percentage):	Roman Catholic (79%) Russian Orthodox (4.1%) Protestant (1.9%) other (5.5%) none (9.5%)
Type of government:	parliamentary democracy
Military service:	19–26 years of age for **compulsory** military service and 18 years of age for volunteers
National coat of arms:	a knight in armor holding a sword and shield, astride a horse

Highest mountains:	Aukštojas Hill in the Medininkai Highlands at 964 feet (294 meters)
Lakes:	Lake Druksiai is largest at 13.9 square miles (36.12 square kilometers) Lake Tauragnas is deepest at 198.5 feet (60.5 meters)
Currency:	*litas* (Lt)
Natural resources:	timber, minerals, agricultural products, **amber**
Major industries:	electric motors, televisions, fridges, freezers, furniture, small ships, amber jewelry
Main exports (percentage):	mineral products (22%) machinery and equipment (10%) chemicals (9%) textiles (7%) foodstuffs (7%) plastics (7%) all other (38%)
Units of measurement:	metric
Internet access in rural areas:	16%
Internet access in city areas:	40%

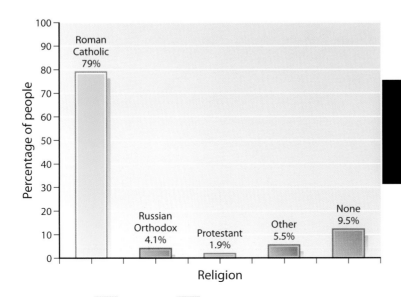

This bar graph shows the different religious groups in Lithuania.

Lithuania's national anthem

Lithuania's national anthem is *Tautiška giesmė* (The National Hymn). It was written in 1898, when Lithuania was part of the Russian Empire. It calls for Lithuanians to take pride in their **heritage** and be good citizens.

Lithuania, our homeland,
Land of heroes!
Let your sons draw their strength
From our past experience
Let your children always follow
Only roads of virtue,
May your own, mankind's well-being
Be the goals they work for
May the sun above our land
Banish darkening clouds around
Light and truth all along
Guide our steps forever
May the love of Lithuania
Brightly burn in our hearts.
For the sake of this land
Let unity blossom

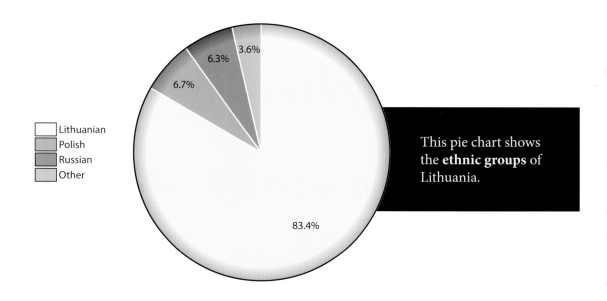

Lithuanian
Polish
Russian
Other

3.6%
6.3%
6.7%
83.4%

This pie chart shows the **ethnic groups** of Lithuania.

The Lithuanian calendar

The Lithuanian calendar is quite unusual. The months' names are not based on mythology. Instead, they celebrate the natural world. Three months are named after birds, two are named after trees, and the others are named after different features of the seasons:

Month	Lithuanian name	Meaning
January	Sausis	dry
February	Vasaris	summer
March	Koyas	rook or struggle
April	Balandis	dove
May	Geyezė	cuckoo
June	Birželis	birch
July	Liepa	linden tree
August	Rugpjūtis	rye
September	Rugsėjis	sow
October	Spalis	flax
November	Lapkritis	leaf fall
December	Gruodis	frozen clod

The days of the week are simply "first day," "second day," and so on, and their names in Lithuanian are: *pirmadienis, antradienis, trečiadienis, ketvirtadienis, penktadienis, šeštadienis*, and *sekmadienis*.

Timeline

BCE is short for before the Common Era. BCE is added after a date and means that the date occurred before the birth of Jesus Christ, for example, 450 BCE.

CE is short for Common Era. CE is added after a date and means that the date occurred after the birth of Jesus Christ, for example, 720 CE.

600–100 BCE	First tribes settle in the area
1200s CE	Mindaugas unites the separate tribes
1253	Mindaugas is crowned king on July 6, which is still celebrated today as the Day of Lithuanian Statehood
1316–1341	Reign of King Gediminas
1387	Christianity arrives in Lithuania
1386	Lithuania's king also becomes king of Poland
1569	The Union of Lublin creates a Polish-Lithuanian state
1579	Vilnius University is founded
1795	Lithuania becomes part of the Russian Empire
1831	Vilnius Univeristy is shut down by the Russians; Roman Catholic churches are closed
1914–1918	World War I takes place; Germany invades Lithuania
1917	The Russian Empire collapses
1918	World War I ends; Germany is defeated and Lithuania becomes independent
1919	Vilnius University is reopened
1939–1945	World War II takes place

1940	Lithuania becomes part of the **Soviet Union**
1941	Germany invades the Lithuanian Soviet Socialist Republic; the **persecution** of Lithuanian **Jews** begins
1944	The Soviet Union again takes control of Lithuania
1989	Mass protest against Soviet occupation across the Baltic states takes place. French National Geographical Institute declares Lithuania as the center of Europe.
1990	Lithuania declares itself independent
1991	Lithuania is officially declared independent as the Republic of Lithuania on September 6. Lithuania joins the United Nations in September.
1992	Lithuania's **constitution** is agreed upon in October
1993	Lithuania joins the Council of Europe
2001	Lithuania joins the World Trade Organization
2004	Lithuania joins the European Union and **NATO**
2009	Unemployment reaches 14%. Lithuania is named a European Capital of Culture. First woman president, Dalia Grybauskaite, is voted in on December 31.

Glossary

amber orange-red stone used in jewelry

biotechnology science that uses very small living things to make things such as medicine

botanical concerned with plants and vegetation

censor examine and control information

Christian related to the religion based on the teachings of Christ, or a person of that religion

communism social system where all people in a country share work and property. People who practice communism are called communists.

compulsory necessary, required, or demanded

concentration camp prison and death camps where people were sent during World War II

constitution set of basic laws by which a nation, state, or other organization is governed

currency banknotes and coins accepted in exchange for goods and services

deport make someone leave a country

dialect forms of languages that are spoken in specific regions or by specific groups of people

dune mound or hill of sand built up by the action of the wind

economy to do with the money, industry, and jobs in a country

endangered in danger of extinction

equinox time occurring in March and September, when day and night are of equal length

erosion wear away

ethnic group group of people who identify with each other because of their shared race, culture, or religion

euro type of currency used in many European countries

EU (European Union) organization of European countries with shared political and economic aims

fertilizer natural or chemical substances added to soil to make it better for growing plants

fine art art that is practiced and admired for its beauty or significance

game meat of wild animals that are hunted to eat

ghetto area in a city where a minority group lives separately

glacier large masses of ice formed in cold regions from compacted snow that move very slowly down a slope or across land

heritage legacy or tradition

Holocaust mass murder of millions of Jews and other minority groups during World War II

import bring in a product, resource, or service from another country

independence having freedom from outside control

Jew person of the Jewish religion, ethnicity, or culture. Jewish people trace their roots back to the ancient Hebrew people of Israel.

judiciary country's system of courts of law

lagoon shallow area of salty water, separated from the sea by sandbars, coral reefs, or islands

legal having to do with law

medieval relating to the Middle Ages, a period in European history between 500 CE and the 1400s

NATO (North Atlantic Treaty Organization) organization that includes the United States, Canada, and many European countries in which members give each other military help

pagan religion where many different things are worshipped. Paganism is usually the religion that was practiced before Christianity.

persecution when people are unfairly or cruelly treated because of their ethnic group, skin color, religion, or political beliefs

phonetic method of representing speech sounds by symbols

publicity information given out that gets the attention of the public

revolt rise up against a government or other authority

rural in the countryside

rye seeds of the rye grass plant, used for cereal, flour, and other grain products

sacred having to do with religion and being shown great respect

service industry part of a country's economy that provides services such as hotels, shops, and schools for its people

Soviet Union communist state made up of Russia and its former empire, in existence between 1922 and 1991

UN (United Nations) organization of many nations started in 1945 to promote world peace and understanding

World Heritage site place of cultural importance that is protected by a United Nations agency

Find Out More

Books

Bultje, Jan Willem. *Looking at Lithuania*. Minneapolis, MN: Oliver Press, 2006.

Docalavich, Heather. *Lithuania*. Broomall, PA: Mason Crest Publishers, 2005.

Kagda, Sakina, and Zawiah Abdul Latif. *Lithuania*. Tarrytown, NY: Marshall Cavendish Children's Books, 2007.

Kaplan, William, and Shelley Tanaka. *One More Border: The True Story of One Family's Escape from War-Torn Europe*. Toronto: ON: Groundwood Books, 2004.

Zee, Ruth Vander, and Marian Sneider. *Eli Remembers*. Grand Rapids, MI: Eerdmans Books for Young Readers, 2007.

Websites

www.urm.lt/index.php?698797363
This website from the Lithuanian Ministry of Foreign Affairs has a section called "Welcome to Lithuania," where you can find out all sorts of useful things about the country.

www.travel.lt/index.php?lang=2
Visit the website of the official tourism organization for Lithuania, where you can find a huge amount of information about what there is to see and do in the country.

www.way2lithuania.com
Travel Lithuania is a company with useful information for visitors to Lithuania, from activities and events to accommodation.

www.glis.lt/?site=5
The Lithuanian Fund for Nature is a nature conservation group. It supports the sustainable development of Lithuania, and is a partner organization of the World Wide Fund for Nature (WWF).

Places to visit

If you ever get the chance to go to Lithuania, here are just some of the many places you could visit:

The Center of Europe
Lithuanians are very proud that the geographical center of Europe is to be found in their country. Just north of Vilnius, this spot is marked by a column of white granite and the flags of all the countries of Europe.

Presidential Palace, Vilnius
This palace, surrounded by beautiful parks and gardens, dates back to the 1300s. It has housed everyone from archbishops to governors, and was converted into the Presidential Palace in 1997.

Hill of Crosses, Šiauliai
Visit this site, where countless people have come to pray and place a wooden cross. Try to guess how many crosses are there!

Palanga Amber Museum, Palanga
There are over 4,500 pieces of amber in this museum. You can learn all about how amber is formed, collected, and processed. There are some beautiful pieces with insects or plants trapped inside.

Trakai Island Castle
This amazing castle in its fairytale setting contains museums and galleries. It is the site for many festivals and events throughout the year.

The Curonian Spit
Now that you've read all about it (see pages 20–21), why not visit the famous Curonian Spit and see it for yourself? You can go walking, boating, and cycling by the spit.

Topic Tools

You can use these topic tools for your school projects. Trace the map onto a sheet of paper, using the thick black outlines to guide you.

The yellow stripe in the Lithuanian flag stands for golden fields, the sun, light, and goodness. The green stripe stands for the forests and nature, freedom, and hope. The red stripe stands for courage and the blood shed for the nation in wars and struggles of the past. Copy the flag design and then color in your picture. Make sure you use the right colors!

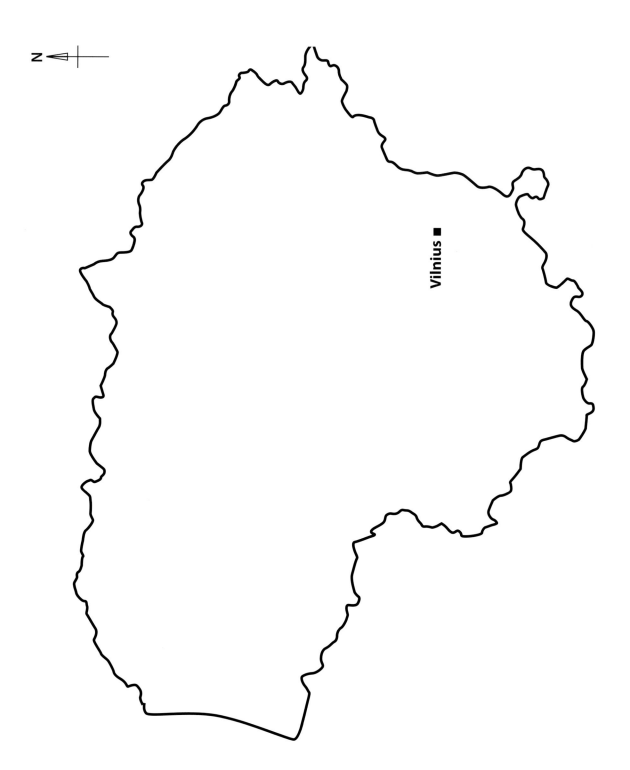

N

Vilnius ■

Index

Titles in the series